INVESTING FOR BEGINNERS

Personal Finance
And Real Estate Investing

By Paul D. Kings
Copyrights 2017 Paul D. Kings

http://bit.ly/pauldkings

No part of this book can be transmitted or reproduced in any form including print, electronic, photocopying, scanning, mechanical or recording without prior written permission from the author.

All information, ideas, and guidelines presented here are for educational purposes only. This book cannot be used to replace information provided with the device. All readers are encouraged to seek professional advice when needed.

Paul D. Kings

TABLE OF CONTENTS

TABLE OF CONTENTS.. 3
WHY YOU SHOULD READ THIS BOOK.. 7
HOW TO PUT THIS BOOK INTO ACTION.. 9
PART I: PERSONAL FINANCE... 11
    Preface for Part I: Personal Finance.................................... 13
CHAPTER 1 - PERSONAL FINANCE.. 17
    What is 'Personal Finance?'.. 17
    Importance of Personal Finance... 19
    The Secret of Sound Financial Planning............................... 25
CHAPTER 2 - PERSONAL FINANCE VS BUSINESS FINANCE........... 27
    Business Finance... 27
    Personal Finance and Accounting... 29
    Balancing Your Account and Personal Finance..................... 30
    Cutting expenses Ideas.. 33
    Generate income Ideas.. 35
CHAPTER 3 - PERSONAL FINANCE AND DEBT............................... 37
    Personal Finance and Debt.. 37
    Tips on Personal Financing and Debt Management............. 39
    How to Get Your Credit Score Under Control....................... 43
    Importance of Budgeting... 45
    Choosing the Best Personal Finance Software..................... 48
PART II: Real Estate Investing... 53
    Preface for Part II: Real Estate Investing............................. 54
CHAPTER 4 - REAL ESTATE BUSINESS.. 55
    Starting a Real Estate Business... 56

Specialty Real Estate Firms...60
Finding the Money to Make Your Dream Happen.........62
Conclusions.. 64

CHAPTER 5 - TIPS FOR MAKING A GOOD REAL ESTATE BUSINESS PLAN..67

Why Invest in Real Estate?..67
Writing An Effective Business Plan................................70

CHAPTER 6 - INVESTING IN COMMERCIAL PROPERTIES 75

Investing in Commercial Property.................................. 75
Tips for Buying Commercial Property............................79
Why Invest in Commercial Properties?......................... 81
Tips on How to Sell Commercial Properties..................84
How to Sell.. 84

CHAPTER 7 - REAL ESTATE AGENTS................................91

Who Are Real Estate Agents?.. 91
What Do Real Estate Agents They Do?..........................92
How Do Real Estate Agents Do Their Job?....................92
Why Should I Use A Real Estate Agent?........................93
What Buyers and Sellers Should Know.........................96
Who Should You Choose to be Your Real Estate Agent? 101
The Problem With Real Estate Agents........................103
How to Look For a Good Real Estate Agent................104
Realtor, Real Estate Agent - is there a difference?.....104
The Search and Some Questions.................................105
Benefits of Using a Real Estate Agent.........................108
Reasons Why You Should Use a Real Estate Agent When Buying a Residential or Commercial property 109

Reasons To Use a Real Estate Agent When Selling Your Home or Commercial property 111
WANT TO LEARN MORE? 115
ABOUT THE AUTHOR 117
ONE LAST THING 119

Paul D. Kings

WHY YOU SHOULD READ THIS BOOK

Do you want to know the secrets to investing? Schools used to teach practical skills such as home economics, workshop, and things that MIGHT have helped you as an adult. With the global economy, everything practical has been pushed out of school and into life.

In school, you're taught a lesson and then given a test. In life, you're given a test that teaches you a lesson.
---Tom Bodett

In this global, 24/7 economy, if you want to get ahead, then you have to teach yourself what others have already learned and what ninety-eight percent of people will be too lazy or oblivious to learning.

Does this mean that you can outwork the majority of people to get ahead? Yes. But you would benefit from merely being able to out-think them, which is *much easier and much more productive.*

Vilfredo Pareto noticed an unequal relationship between inputs (work) and outputs (results). His theory, commonly known as the 80/20 principle, states that 20% of my effort is responsible for 80% of my results. The 20% of the effort you invest should be in optimizing and taking control of four crucial areas of your life: Personal Finance, Real Estate Investing, Money Making Opportunities, and Business Investing.

If you are to get out of your life what you really deserve to receive, you will have to know how to manage:

- Your **personal finances** understanding your cash flow and by creating opportunities to make more money than you spend.
- Your **real estate investing** by knowing when and how to decide to hire a real estate agent and how to do real estate investing on your own.

HOW TO PUT THIS BOOK INTO ACTION...

First, read the whole book, reserving judgment about whether you 'need' that section or not. Maybe you think you don't have the money to invest in real estate, so you may be tempted to skip that section. I say, don't. I know it will plant a seed, which will grow in your future. Besides, if you do even a portion of the things recommended in the other areas of the book, then you will make the money you need to invest in real estate or anything else you decide to do.

Second, highlight the parts you really need to master, so you can easily get back to them. On the Kindle, highlighting is easy, just a swipe of your finger, and then it is importable into your computer as notes. That may be an ideal way to make a 'touch list' out of the information.

Lastly, share this book with a friend so you have someone to talk to about it and who can hold you accountable. If you tell at least one person about what you are learning, not only does it reinforce it in your memory, then you have spoken it into your future. When you know others expect you to keep your promise to do what you need to do, your success rate goes up!

Paul D. Kings

PART I: PERSONAL FINANCE

Paul D. Kings

Preface for Part I: Personal Finance

When we are trying to understand what personal finance actually is, the best thing to do is to understand what personal finance is *not*.

Many people think that accounting and personal finance are the same, but personal finance is *not* accounting. Personal finance is a **strategy** to get money, keep it, or optimize your income. Accounting is counting the money you have or need. On the surface, they may seem the same; they both have to do with money. However, this book will help you better understand the differences and how to go about using the tips and tricks to create a sustainable strategy for personal finance.

Also, you will learn how to manage your accounting in a way that is more effective and streamlined so that will, in turn, lead you to learn how to make sound personal and business financial decisions. The accounting principles that I see most people botch are the little everyday wasteful things which if given a tiny bit more attention could translate to thousands more dollars kept in your bank account per year.

According to The Millionaire Next Door, authored by Thomas J. Stanley:

Prodigious accumulators of wealth spend nearly twice as many hours per month planning their investments as under accumulators of wealth.

What does that mean to you? It means you either plan or strategize your personal finances or you *plan to fail* in your personal finances. That you chose this book means you are ready to do some real planning, adopt a coherent strategy, and create a path to freedom with your personal finances.

Here are the real steps for personal finance success:
First, you have to know where you are. You can't decide if you are where you want to be unless you know where you actually are. So, gathering up all of your financial information is key. Once you have it all together, you will be able to analyze it.

Second, you will need to develop your goal list. You can't decide if you have hit your goals until they are written and you can measure them. You may want to tackle one goal at a time, focusing all your efforts on that one goal until it is accomplished.

Or, you may want to spread your efforts on a number of interlocking goals, such as debt repayment, credit score, and cash flow. Those goals go hand in hand, so the improvement of one necessitates the improvement of the others.

Third, you will need to set up treats or accomplishment rewards for yourself along the way. You can't do this without commitment and change. All of those changes will not be pleasant, but if you have a goal and you reach it, then you deserve to give yourself a treat. For example, if you improve your credit score 50 points, then you get to....(whatever your low budget favorite thing might be).

Fourth, it is about *cash flow*. It won't matter how much you make if you always spend more. So income has to exceed expenses. Your income probably won't exceed your expenses for a while, but moving from a negative cash flow to a positive cash flow is an incremental planned strategy. If you are spending $1500 more per month than you make, the next goal would be to spend only $750 more per month than you make. Then the next goal might be to spend only $350 more per month than you make, and so on. This will take a very rigorous and detailed look at ways to make more money and to spend less money. Not all of them will be pleasant or fun.

Finally, the end result should be getting from a negative net worth to a positive net worth. Put simply, net worth is the value of what you own or control minus what you owe someone else for it. *Positive Net worth* is the indicator that you have put your financial house in order. This is how you will know that you are THERE...that you have done what ninety-eight percent of the population of planet Earth have not and will not do. Net worth is the single number that tells you that your total personal finance strategy is working, or not working.

CHAPTER 1 - PERSONAL FINANCE

What is 'Personal Finance?'

Personal finance encompasses all the financial decisions and activities of an individual or household, to create, budget, save and spend money, including goal budgeting, credit score management, insurance coverage, mortgage planning, savings in the short term and long term, retirement planning, estate tax and will planning.

Managing your money and personal finances is simple with just a basic understanding of the world of finance. Notice that I didn't say *easy*. It is simple, but it is not easy. With the local and global pressures upon you to bend to the advertisers and to spend money before you have it…it will never be easy. But, you can learn to handle yourself in stressful moments with this guide to personal finances, budgeting money, managing personal finances, using personal budget software or seeking finance help online. This financial guide offers great value in assisting you in all areas of money.

You will either understand your money or you will be controlled by it. The choice seems clear.

Most people don't think of themselves, or their lives, as a business. Yet from birth to passing, you are in business for yourself, essentially the business of you. Unless you are on a trust fund, how you choose to manage your business is up to you. The same guidelines that apply to running a successful business also apply to leading a victorious life, both financially with your money and feeling emotionally free.

Instead of wondering when your next vacation is, maybe you should set up a life you don't need to escape from.
— Seth Godin

Remember, stress around money can affect your emotions negatively, as well as your health and most of those ninety-eight percent of people who would not be reading this book are stressed to the max and wishing for any type of escape from their lives, whether it be the weekend or a vacation.

Another aspect of personal finance that may alleviate your feeling that this is all about greed, which is giving adequate service to our fellow human beings, as well as providing value to their lives. If you seek to provide as much value to as many human beings in your life, you are sure to become a successful person where customers and wealth will knock at your door. So how does this apply to managing finances successfully you might ask?

Importance of Personal Finance

Personal Finance is the application of a *strategy* of financial principles to the financial decisions made by a family unit or an individual. It addresses many facts of financial issues, such as creating a budget, including evaluating cash flow, how to save, reducing financial risks, and how to spend your monetary resources over a long term plan.

Truly, really rich people, those who would probably not be reading this book are taught by their parents that to have true financial wealth you have to stretch the money over three generations or more. So, when speaking of a long term plan, don't just think of your lifetime. Think of the lifetimes which would be encompassed by will planning, to leave something to your next generation and many generations to come.

In the world we live today, personal finance and planning is no longer the luxury of the rich, but has become a necessary part of life. Preparing for one's future is essential, and there is never a good time to start like today.

To many people, the thought of Personal Finance is like speaking language from Mars to them, and they have no clue where to start. It can be mind boggling when terms like budgets, balance sheets, and income statements are spoken.

However this should not sound an alarm, since most of us engage in personal finance decisions without knowing it. For instance, when making decisions of where to live, which car to buy, where to take your children to school, among others. These decisions have a factor of finance involved in them somewhere.

There is an emergence of personal finance advisors in the recent past, who have come up to assist people who need coaching or financial advice for a fee. They come in handy, especially for those of us who don't have strong financial background and require help.

Whether you choose to do it yourself, or get the help of a personal finance advisor, there are some common basic things that one needs to look at. The order of these may vary from person to person or from one advisor to another.

To begin with, one needs to look at their current financial position. That is to say, take an honest look at what you owe, and what you own (your quick snapshot of your net worth). Then you proceed on to setting your financial goals, both in the short term and in the long term. You may think in the lines of the kind of lifestyle you want to have in the future.

Finally, and most importly, is to come up with a strategy, or a road map, that will help you achieve the financial goals set and follow them through. This could include saving and investing a portion of your income, for example.

One another thing that one needs to consider is the tax element, depending on which country you live in. Tax can be a major expense that most people never give a second thought to, thus ending up missing out on opportunities they have to reduce it.

Since taxes can be anywhere from ten to fifty percent of your income, it is an important area to have a strategy. Most tax regimes have some incentives or relief to give to the tax payer to encourage them to save or to invest in certain things. For instance, payments made towards retirement, life insurance or specific purchases, such as buying a home through a mortgage. It would be prudent to investigate the possible saving available to you from a tax perspective.

Whichever way you look at personal finance, it is vital for every one of us to take charge of our finances by avoiding common pitfalls that many have endured, because they never take time to consciously look at their personal finance. Are you going to leave your finances to fate? Or are you taking charge of your financial destiny today? The choice is yours.

Below are 4 important points to managing personal finances successfully.

Take extra effort in removing any emotion, like debt anxiety, or overwhelm from financial obligations worry over mounting bills and income. Removing the emotion from your personal finance budgeting will be a work in progress, and you should always remain on guard for over-active emotions. Taking emotion out of dealing with your finances will help you come up with positive solutions and solve problems more effectively.

Managing your personal finances on a regular basis, rather than letting the tasks mount up, is important. That way you stay on top of where you are and can change things as you go along. Make better decisions ahead of time rather than always being in reaction mode or putting out fires. Avoid decisions that would lead to bankruptcy, like over leveraging your loans or, taking on financial commitments you don't know how you can pay back.

Devote yourself to develop greater skill sets, like budgeting, planning, and even using budgeting software. Managing personal finances like a business are about seizing control of your destiny, both with your finances, and your life.

The software that could get you started, which is highly recommended by many financial gurus is the FREE program https://www.mint.com/
It is an online software from Intuit, the makers of Quickbooks. Yes, it has lots of ways that they want you to save money through their products, but the simple use of the software is useful and free. It will give you instant, up to the minute information about your budget, goals, income, net worth, etc.

You can connect Mint to all of your bank accounts, credit cards, student loans, car loans, real estate, etc. You can connect everything you own and everyone you owe to it and it will put at your fingertips the most important information in different graphs that you could imagine.

Try to be like the great business leaders, and attack your future with vigor and enthusiasm. Overseeing your finances in this way, with boldness, and a belief in their importance, can have amazing results. Lead the way to conquering your money with a spirit of boldness, and your army of your personal finances are sure to follow that leadership.

Using this software to support you with your personal budgeting is a good idea because it contains trigger alerts which can email you when you are close to your budget in a certain category. You can see very quickly where your current expenses are, budget better, plan better, not to mention the time it will save you putting your own spreadsheet together and updating it.

Using a personal finance software provides sufficient user-friendly features, allowing you to manage every aspect of your finances, including accounts, investments, future plans, and taxes. Software will provide up to date information on tax laws and stock reviews to help you make knowledgeable decisions.

The Secret of Sound Financial Planning

Having a good personal finance guide is very necessary in relation to the financial industry as we know it today. There are numerous online guides, books, and YouTube videos to help you cope with the current economic instability. Below are some helpful tips to guide you to a healthier financial situation.

First, a well planned budget is the beginning of any financial plan. You need something to help your spending and personal finances stay on track to reach your financial goals. A budget will outline expenses, payments, and ideally include savings and your plan to pay back credit cards and loans you are obligated to.

Second, your budget will help you cut back on unnecessary expenses which is the next step to sound financial management. This might mean eating out less, using your ceiling fans more instead of your central air conditioning, and for others, it could mean getting rid of that extra motor vehicle. Whatever the case may be, everyone has an area or two where money can be saved by reducing some basic expenses.

Third, keep a savings account where you pay yourself first. You want to ideally start with saving 10% of everything you earn. If you can't do that right now, it is best to start the habit of putting something aside each time money comes in, even if it is just $1.

Fourth, cut up your store cards. Don't close the accounts, because that can hurt your credit score. You want to pay them down and not use them, but not cancel the accounts entirely. The interest is too high and encourages unnecessary and impulse spending. Consolidate your credit card interest to just two credit cards, if you must. Keep one for typical use, and the other one clear for emergencies.

One main part of decreasing expenses is to slow down or stop paying to use other people's money, which is credit. Credit is a modern way of establishing a debtor's prison. Very easily, with little effort, you can be in debt enough to have to work years to pay it off. If you are going to use credit, it is best to obtain education on the matter so you are in touch with how much interest you will pay if you keep a number of store cards and credit cards on hand. Some form of education should be undertaken so one can avoid the dangers of unwise credit decisions. Following a personal finance guide will keep you on financial track.

CHAPTER 2 - PERSONAL FINANCE VS BUSINESS FINANCE

Business Finance

Business finance is a term that encompasses a wide range of activities and disciplines revolving around the management of money, and other valuable assets related to an enterprise which makes you money, your business.

Business finance programs in universities familiarize students with accounting methodologies, investing strategies and effective debt management. Small business owners must have a solid understanding of the principles of finance to keep their companies profitable.

When starting a business, one of the biggest things you must make sure you have control over, and have a plan for, is your finances. Do you make a budget with your personal finances and stick to it? If not, you should. Have you created a financial plan for your personal finances, as well as your business finances? They should be separate but related to each other, using the same principles with both.

It only takes a small leak to sink a great ship. Your business is like a great ship you have crafted, and it will sail you to the ends of the world if properly constructed and well maintained. Even a small flaw such as going over budget, or not setting a plan and sticking to it can lead to financial disaster.

If you are not able to keep a budget and stick to it, or layout a financial plan and stick to it as well, how do you think you will do while running a business? The point here is not to discourage you from following your dreams. However, you must understand that if you have a problem managing your own finances, you will probably run into the same sort of problems down the road with your business.

If you have problems with your personal finances, that is okay, you just need to realize the importance of figuring out what those problems are, and find a way to solve them. There are many articles and books on the subject of money management and budgeting. The first step towards recovery is realizing and accepting that there is a problem. When you realize there is a problem you can seek out ways to solve it.

So start now, don't wait. Sit down tonight and make a list of your personal finances, figure out exactly how much money to spend and how much money to save, and stick to it and improve where you see fit.

Personal Finance and Accounting

Merriam-Webster's definition of accounting is, "the system of recording and summarizing business and financial transactions and analyzing, verifying, and reporting the results." Based on this definition, we see that accounting is the process of analysing and recording what you have already done with your money. This is why having an accountant is usually not enough when it comes to your personal finances. Accountants generally don't concern themselves with personal finance—although there are some exceptions to this rule.

Unless your accountant is also a financial advisor or coach, he or she will likely just look at what you have done with your money at the end of the year, and provide you with a report of their analysis. This report is usually your tax return; what you owe the government or what the government owes you. Very rarely does the accountant provide an individual with a Balance Sheet or Income Statement or a Net worth statement; all very helpful tools that are necessary to effectively manage your personal finances.

Personal Finance is looking at your finances from a more pro-active and goal oriented perspective. This is what provides the accountants with something to record, verify, and analyze.

The Merriam-Webster's—*Concise Encyclopedia*—definition of "Finance" is the *"process of raising funds or capital for any kind of expenditure. Consumers, business firms, and governments often do not have the funds they need to make purchases or conduct their operations, while savers and investors have funds that could earn interest or dividends if put to productive use. Finance is the process of channeling funds from savers to users in the form of credit, loans, or invested capital through agencies including commercial banks, savings, and loan associations, and such non-bank organizations as Credit Unions and investment companies. Finance can be divided into three broad areas: Business finance, personal finance, and public finance. All three involve generating budgets and managing funds for the optimum results."*

Balancing Your Account and Personal Finance

It is certainly a rarity to see someone at the store using cash to pay for their items. Even rarer would be to come across an establishment that only accepted cash as a type of payment. Americans today prefer the quick and easy swipe of a credit/debit card. However, this convenience can come with a price to your personal finances.

The literal "price" of over-drafting with a debit card can be up to $36 per overdraft, and with the economy and banking laws rapidly changing, fees are rising swiftly. Unpaid overdraft fees reflect negatively on your credit score, and even paid ones can affect your banks likelihood to lend to you. Not to mention, according to a Dunn and Bradstreet study, Americans spend up to 18% more when they swipe, which heavily influences their personal finances.

Overall, if you are like most people who regularly choose a card over any other type of payment, then it is vital to conscientiously handle your personal finances. A sensible place to begin is with the simple habit of asking for, and saving, receipts.

The receipts will show you where that mysterious "18%" is going, and will aid you while you are balancing your account. Some people find it helpful to go through and write down the receipts nightly, while others sufficiently run their personal finances by keeping the receipts in a envelope until the end of the week. Reading over receipts will also help you write an accurate budget as you learn the truth about where your money is going.

However, debit transactions are not the only transactions going in and out of an individual's account, due to the fact that many people set up automatic withdrawal for monthly bills like mortgage, car insurance, and utilities. To correctly keep track of your personal finances, you must use every means of account balancing possible to go along with old fashioned pen and paper, which includes online and phone banking.

Luckily, many banks are now offering these amenities for free. Helpful tellers and self-explanatory websites make online banking easy and enjoyable, while simple codes and instructions cause phone banking to be a easy means of checking your account.

To properly balance your account and control your personal finances, devote time weekly, if not daily, to comparing and contrasting your receipts to your online information, and the information you hear through the phone. It is important to check both because they are not updated simultaneously. Many times the services will be updated days apart and may not post new transaction on the weekends. Your pen and paper account will come in very handy on Friday when you know you will not have precise account information until Monday.

Following these simple steps will positively impact your personal finances, and lead you to feel more in control of your account. If you know what has come in (income) and what is going out (expenses), then you can calculate your cash flow. If your expenses are higher than your income, your cash flow will be negative. The first goal is to get the number figured out. The second would be to tighten down from a negative cash flow to a positive one.

Cutting expenses Ideas

Carpool to work, which cuts down on many expenses and encourages you to take your lunch with you because you won't have your car to zip over and get convenience foods.

Every six months, call ALL of your credit card companies and ask them for an interest reduction, a higher balance, and no annual fees (if applicable). This will increase your credit score by leaps and bounds. It doesn't mean you will use that higher balance if it is available; it means that it will increase your credit score and let them decrease your interest rates.

Consolidate your student loans and if they are at a low-interest rate, ask for a forbearance or other delay in paying them so you can concentrate on your high-interest credit cards. Always pay the highest interest rate first...and most.

Credit card balance transfers can be awesome or they can be a trap. If you have self-control and are paying attention, you can pay down high-interest cards while your other debt is on a low or zero interest card and you are paying the minimum. If you can't control yourself or think you may spend the available balance, keep it where it is.

Cut expenses in the following areas: energy costs, entertainment, travel, subscriptions, Netflix vs Amazon Prime, cook and pack your own meals, raise your deductibles on your insurance, optimize your cell or cable bill, stop buying clothing (you have more than enough).

Generate income Ideas

Sell some stuff, your garage full of stuff or just some antiques or just some collectibles. If you get radical, have an 'estate' sale in your house. Invite an auctioneer to sell half of your stuff. Your house will be cleaner, you will have less stuff to move, dust, and maintain...and you will have money.

Get a side GIG, such as:
- Provide rides via Uber, Lyft, or other companies.
- Rent out your own car via Getaround and Relayrides
- Rent rooms in your house via Airbnb, VRBO or HomeAway.
- Be a dog sitter via Rover and DogVacay.
- Freelance work such as writing, wedding photography, nanny or babysit.
- Sell items you make through Etsy or Amazon Handmade, Launch an online course, or give lessons in person in a musical instrument or skill.
- Offer handyman or handywoman skills to neighbors.
- Lead Fitness Boot Camps.
- Offer any other skill or resource that you have to make up the difference between what you owe and what you make per month.

Paul D. Kings

CHAPTER 3 - PERSONAL FINANCE AND DEBT

Personal Finance and Debt

Personal finances may spiral out of control if they are not managed properly. A small and innocent little loan such as a credit card debt can become a huge loan if payments are not made on time. This is a common problem that is encountered by many consumers, especially among new credit users that may not understand compound interest. If no attention is paid to the matter, the situation will only go from bad to worse. Let's take a look at how this could happen.

When an individual first starts out in a job, he will be receiving a monthly pay check. For the average person, the pay check is perhaps the biggest sum of money that they have seen. When they got the pay check, the very first thing they did was to go out and spend the money.

Usually, the money is not spent wisely. Instead, it's spent on goods and services that are not essential items. For example, going for a drinking session and ending up footing the bill for a group of friends. That will easily amount to a few hundred dollars for a single night.

The bill is charged to the credit card. As no real money is exchanged, it is very hard to track the spending. Soon, using credit cards for purchases will become a habit. When the bill comes for the card payments, the individual realizes that they don't have enough to cover all the bills. So they pay the minimum amount required and let the balance be carried over to the next bill.

Then the next bill arrives, but it's even worse this time. On top of the current month's spending, they know they have to pay previous month's payments, plus interest. In few month's time, the payment amounts would have added up to such huge amounts, that it's beyond the individual's ability to clear the debts.

So where does it all start? It all starts with not having enough to pay the first payment. In other words, overspending is the problem at hand here. If the monthly payments are paid on time, the debt would have remained reasonably small and manageable.

To make things worse, some people sign up for multiple credit cards. When they hit the credit limit for one card, they just start using another card. Having many different cards enables a person to take on multiple loans. On top of credit card loans, there are other loans that an individual may need to take care of. For example, there may be student loans, mortgage loans, car loans, etc.

Tips on Personal Financing and Debt Management

If you are in debt, you need to reduce and eventually clear your debt first before anything else is done to improve your financial outlook. The key to debt reduction and elimination is your own commitment and discipline. Basically, you have to make more than you spend. That's going to mean a lot of little changes, some of which will be easy, others will be embarrassing, and yet others may be painful. The steps for debt reduction and elimination are very simple, but not easy. The challenge is to stay the course and manage your emotions about your money.

Stop Further Debt

Excessive borrowing is the cause of most debt problems. You should only borrow what you really need. Keeping proper records of your debt and do not lose sight of your objectives. Your debt should be for the short term, and you should aim to clear them within a few months. Do not let your loans balloon into an out of control debt problem.

Reduce Your Expenditures

Make this an obsession. If you take the bus or train to work instead of driving, congratulate yourself on the money you are saving on gas and parking. If you have packed lunch instead of spending money at the cafeteria or expensive restaurant, congratulate yourself. You would have saved up to $3000 a year. Money that will go a long way to reducing your debt.

Reduce Your Debt

Try to consolidate your debts and secure a lower interest rate. Call each credit card company every six months to ask for a lower interest rate. They will lower your interest ONLY if you ask, and they will do it based on your payment history. They look back the past six months, so if you have been paying on time and paying more than the minimum amount, they will decrease your interest, sometimes 1-2% on your annual percentage rate.

That doesn't sound like much, but when you look at the monthly interest, compounded interest, measured over several cards, it can be a significant saving. Start paying more than the minimum sum and set a target date to clear your debt. This is the only way to reduce your debts. To achieve this, you need a proper budget.

Make a Monthly Budget

One of the most effective and important money management tools is your budget. Coming up with a budget is fairly simple but you need to have the discipline to stick to it. A budget is simply a schedule of your earning and what you need to spend. The key words here are "what you need to spend."

Be prudent and frugal with your money, you are already in debt, what other reason do you need? The key to good personal finance management is to spend within your means. To curb impulse spending, try leaving your credit cards at home.

Get Into a Debt Settlement Program

If you have a huge debt, usually thought of as more than 30 percent of your annual salary, think about getting into a debt settlement program. If you want to do it yourself, you just need to contact your creditors to inform them about your plan for debt settlement.

Most financial institutions are open to a debt settlement proposal so you should not hesitate to ask them for better terms. Most financial companies will allow up to 40% to 60% reduction on loans amount payable under special circumstances.

Negotiations can be quite tricky, so you can consider hiring a debt settlement company if you are not up to it. Most of the time, they need to be convinced that you are nearing the teetering edge of bankruptcy and 40-60% is better than the 0% they would get if you went bankrupt.

Proper personal finance and debt management will allow you to get ahead in life. So make sure you are dedicated and motivated to do what it takes in order to provide a sound financial life for yourself and your family.

How to Get Your Credit Score Under Control

If you are in debt, you might be worried about your credit score. Even if you only owe $2,000 to your credit card companies, which you are behind on paying, you might have a lower credit score and then higher interest on the next thing you want to borrow. So, it bites you twice!

Many Americans go through life content with driving a car that gets them from point A to point B. Many Americans are also content on renting an apartment their entire lives. You might be different.

You might be interested in buying a home, getting a new car, or you might realize that there could be a time when you need to borrow money for personal reasons. As you know, you can't do these things when you have a bad credit score or it will cost you many times over in interest. Lots of companies specialize in loaning to those who have bad credit, but the interest rates are astronomical.

Are you looking for few ways to get your personal finances and your debt under control? If so, you have a number of options. Now, before we get started, know that there is a big difference between owing $2,000 in debt and owing $20,000. It is really about debt to income ratio. If you have an income of $100,000 per year and you owe $2,000, then you are doing fine. If your income is $10,000 and you owe $2,000, then you are drowning in debt. So, do the math and figure out what your debt to income ratio is.

If you owe just a tiny bit of money to your creditors, it is recommended that you start by creating a detailed budget for yourself. This budget will total up your monthly necessary expenses, such as rent or your mortgage and establish a savings plan. Also, you will want to track your spending when out and about. This means writing down everything, even small expenses. After a week or so, look at your spending habits. Lets say that you owe that $2,000 still. If you were able to trim your budget by $15 a week, this makes you that much closer to getting out of debt.

As previously stated, there is a difference between owing a little bit of money and a massive amount of money. So lets say that you owe $20,000. If you were only able to trim your spending by $15 a week, it would take you a lifetime to make any impact on the amount! The thing here though is that I bet you could easily trim your spending more than $15 a week, but you need to know where to look.

That is why it is recommended that consumers who are massively in debt seek professional help. If you want to eliminate what you owe, or consolidate your bills, then debt settlement and consolidation are best.

If you'd like helpful advice on what to do next with your personal finances or how to save money, you want to seek help from a credit counselor or a financial planner.

There has really never been a more advantageous time for consumers to try and eliminate unsecured debt. Creditors are very concerned about collecting, and most have government money to make eliminating some of your debt financially feasible.

Importance of Budgeting

In order to get rid of debt, regardless of the method you use to get out of debt, the most crucial thing you can do is to budget! If you are struggling with debt, or wish to have a better financial handle on your life, then don't overlook the importance of budgeting with a WRITTEN plan.

If you already have the habit of tracking your expenses, then congratulations, you are a step ahead of most people already! If you have never kept a budget, or have tried, but easily lose track of or forget about documenting your expenses, then now is the time to start, or change the system of budgeting you use. The more automatic the system, the more likely you are to use it to the best advantage. That's why a software will be able to send you alerts or keep you on track better than a spreadsheet.

A good budget should include expenses, be realistic when setting your expenses, not going too low or too high in any area. Usually, I recommend that you go with what you spend in average over the past three months minus 10%. That is realistic and sustainable. Each quarter, you go down another 10% until you are balanced or below your income.

The budget should also include your earnings, as an average, so if your income fluctuates from month to month you can compensate. There are many ways to track a budget. Choose the method that works best for you, your situation, and lifestyle.

Examples of some systems to use include: downloading an app on your phone, meticulously recording everything you spend, as well as all income that you receive. If you are not that excited about apps or they crash your phone, you can use your phone's memo function as well to notate purchases.

You can use software on your computer like excel or some other data recording program, and there are budgeting phone apps that you can download. I use this method for the convenience and ease of use it provides. The good old envelope system may work well for some people too, where you withdraw cash each month, put the cash in labeled envelopes, you then use the cash from the envelopes with no record taking needed.

There are many ways you can keep a budget. The important thing is to find a method that fits your personality, or play around with the different ways to budget, and then stick to what works best for you.

Remember, this is an acquired skill for most people, so don't get discouraged or give up. Just continue to strive, maintain your focus, and soon you will be able to save more money, get rid of debt, and more importantly, stay out of debt.

Choosing the Best Personal Finance Software

In any purchasing decision you make in life you must match your needs with the features of the product you are purchasing, in order to make the best decision. This also applies when you are investing in personal finance software. You don't want to invest in a package that is too complex for your needs or has functions that you will never need to use in the future.

Having gone online to research the best software packages on a well known retail site, I analysed two categories in the following categories:

Software > Business and Office > Personal Finance and Tax

Software >Home computing > Personal Finance and Tax

I then looked at the best sellers, and in my mind, I was going to review software packages about personal finance. However, when the product features mentioned "creating invoices" and "tracking sales" I suddenly realized that this was not the software that I sought. This software was very much geared to accounting or book keeping. Therefore the category above business and office does not seem the appropriate category.

I then decided to go back to basics and look up the definition of personal finance, which is, "the application of the principles of finance to the monetary decisions of an individual or family unit."

Tracking sales and creating invoices would be associated with a small business carried out by a sole proprietor or a partnership. The category of "tax" was added to the personal finance category meaning that accounting and self assessment software would be included in this category.

Therefore it is very important to check thoroughly what your needs are, before investing in personal finance software. You don't want to invest in a package that is too complex for your needs, or has functions that you will never need to use in the future.

You should take the following steps:

1. List down the reasons why you need the software.

The following hypothetical list is an example of reasons to buy software:
- Keeping track of bank accounts, credit cards and loans, and savings.
- Keeping track of investments i.e. the stock market, bonds, and mutual funds
- Keeping track of insurance, i.e. life insurance and health insurance.
- Monitoring of individual or company provided retirement plans.
- Income tax management.
- Monitoring standing orders and direct debits.
- Budgeting and planning for future spending.

2. Cross check the list in 1 above with what the various software packages have to offer, and come up with a best fit.

3. Read reviews on the products that you have chosen in 2 above, and chose one package based on the best ratings.

If you follow the points above you will end up buying a personal finance software package that is specifically tailored to your needs and more than likely give you value for money. Therefore you must look before you leap.

There are many free programs, which may be fine to get you started. When you are going from nothing to something, you must be able to really use it or it won't give you accurate information. Start out simple and you can get more complex as you create good financial management habits.

If you use a software program, not only is there not a bunch of boring math to do, it is like playing a video game. You make a change, then see how it gets reflected in the numbers. And it makes seeing the hard changes in your lifestyle a little bit more palatable.

Paul D. Kings

PART II: Real Estate Investing

Preface for Part II: Real Estate Investing

Real estate has always been known as one of the safest of investments. Most of the wealth that most people have is centered in their real estate. If you can figure out how to do it well, there is a gold mine waiting for you. In fact, real estate investment completed after proper research into and evaluation of the property (to determine actual and future value), can lead to tremendous profit. This is one reason many people choose real estate investment as their full time job.

Discussions about real estate tend to focus on residential real estate. There are great opportunities to be had, the skill set needed is low, and the money expenditure is manageable. That's why it is usually the training wheels version of real estate investment.

Commercial real estate, because it is more capital outlay at once is usually only done by more seasoned investors. However, commercial real estate is also a great option for investing in real estate. Read this book to learn everything you need to know about real estate and the best approach to investing in commercial properties.

CHAPTER 4 - REAL ESTATE BUSINESS

Unlike most other businesses, a real estate business is a venture that has no bounds provided if you have the right skills and financial back-up. You can even start from smaller property transactions to upgrade yourself to business tycoons within a short time span if you possess the right attitude. All you have to do is incorporate some business skills and develop effective marketing.

Once you are into this business, you can set your own work and time schedule, develop your own marketing methods, find a suitable client base and flourish in the business on your own. The main attraction in this business is, you are the boss.

You have the liberty of taking decisions and authority of trying innovative techniques as per your imagination. Once you have found a person working in the similar field with a matching stream of your thoughts, you can work together towards better results.

This business offers a huge potential for your growth from a single entity controlled business to a large business firm. In this business, investment of your time is the major factor that influences your revenue.

If it is possible for you to employ few assistants; it can produce evident results in your business within a short time. Once you are into the business, you have to determine what you have to spend on marketing and plan strategies within your particular budget of time and money. You have to take care of certain things and do a little research on the topic before you start a new venture in real estate.

If you look at the different types like residential, commercial, land, industrial, institutional and investment that you can trade with, you will be able to notice that most new comers into this business opt to deal with residential and vacant land type of real estate. This is because residential land purchasing contributes to a large chunk of the whole business. New comers find this is an easy pick to survive in the business until they are established. It is easy to buy a spot of land, put a quick structure on it and have a rental for cash flow.

Starting a Real Estate Business

The real estate industry is very sensitive to economic changes like interest rates and the cost of materials in building houses. Interest rates in particular can easily swing the number of sales that are completed during any quarter of the year. Rising interest rates will slow down the sales and falling rates will aid the sales of the real estate. This is an important fact in the real estate business as this can absolutely cause rapid changes in income from the sales that can be made.

With this in mind, the time to buy an agency that comes up for sale may be when the real estate business is in the doldrums. These super-slumps of real estate happen every 15-20 years like clockwork. Since we just experienced one of these almost cataclysmic slumps in 2007, we are due for a housing bubble bursting between 2021-2026. A hot real estate market will make an existing firm worth more, as their income will be higher during this period of time and they will have less incentive to get out. Of course, if you follow this course of action, you will have to wait out the slow down in the markets.

Another factor in the purchase or start-up of a real estate company is the state licensing requirements. You can either become a real estate broker or pay a broker to head your agency.

Most states have serious requirements for real estate agents and brokers. Brokers have much stiffer requirements in most states than an agent. The requirements include passing exams and a fixed number of educational hours for both agents and brokers. There is also requirement for continuing education.

You would either hire a broker or become a broker, with these state mandated steps being met before an agency could be purchased or started. Since this industry is regulated and has strong legal steps to comply with, this licensing plus experience would be an initial step to being a owner in this field. This is not a business that can be stepped into by just paying out some money.

An agent can have the goal of owning their own firm, but it will take planning and meeting the state rules to make this happen. Once a potential owner has these steps out of the way, finding a existing business to buy will be in order.

A quick check of real estate business listings reveals that they are usually found in larger cities and the asking price is significant. There are also resales of franchise companies.

Just typing into a search engine, "Real estate businesses for sale" will come up with many opportunities. A buyer could also check with business brokers and real estate brokers in their city because they would know what is coming up for sale before it makes it to the official market. Another source worth checking out would be a franchise connection, which can be bought for very little per month.

An ongoing real estate business has advantages, as the name is already known and will get clients due to this. When you start a company from the ground up you do not have this advantage. An existing business with several locations will come with a higher price tag than what you could start your own business for.

Another way to gain ownership would be buying into a existing business, beginning as an investment partner as you learn the business alongside its day to day management concerns. This could work if you have a solid relationship with the current owner. The problem is you will not have the final say in most decisions unless you are buying controlling interest in the firm. In a Limited Liability Partnership, because the current owner is likely the Broker of Record, then the legal responsibilities of the transactions are on them. You would only be liable for any legal concerns related to the business management, limited to the amount you have invested.

Specialty Real Estate Firms

Most people think about a firm that helps with the buying and selling of residential homes. There are several other areas of specialization. Real estate firms could become expert in buying and selling commercial property, farmland and farms, farm product processing plants, bank owned properties, government owned properties (Housing and Urban Development or Veterans Affairs), distressed properties (such as short sales, tax deed sales, foreclosures), rental investment properties, and shopping centers.

A sub-specialty is residential or commercial property management, which has its own set of rules and liabilities. There are so many opportunities to be chosen from that you could become an expert in one or more of these areas and create a substantial empire from them.

Actually a real estate broker could cut out a niche market available in any of the types of real estate business. For example, you could specialize in commercial shopping malls. If you are in an area where enough of them are being bought and sold, you could become the expert in that niche and corner the market.

Because commercial real estate has fewer people specializing in it, the rules are more permissive for the brokers who wade in, for example, you can work both sides of the transaction in many cases. If you have an area of expertise, this could become something that could be marketable and cut out a lot of competition in certain situations.

Some real estate firms have unique departments that handle certain types of real estate marketing, such as:

- Residential Properties
- Commercial Properties
- Property Management
- Auctioned Properties
- Foreclosed Properties
- Bank-Owned Properties
- Distressed Properties
- HUD-Owned Properties
- etc.

The decision you must make will determine what kind of a firm are you going to own or be a partner with. You may have to start your own in order to make it happen and starting small will help you learn the business from the ground up.

You could also get into real estate management and the buying and selling of these rental properties, which is a very unique part of the industry. Shopping center related firms could be in from the start of a project. They can help with the formation of the firm to build and own the property and then handle the rentals and day-to-day management of the center.

The point of all of this is there are areas of real estate specialization that lend themselves to a business that just works in this real estate category. Once you decide what you want to be an expert in, then you can choose your business model and make it happen.

Finding the Money to Make Your Dream Happen

You may not have the total purchase price for an existing business. The question is how do you come up with the balance to make the deal. Finding a source to lend you the money is one way to come up with the needed funds.

There are businesses that offer loans to new owners of businesses. These can be found on the Internet by just doing a search. Family and friends could be another source of money. One way to get the needed money is to create a partnership for the business. If you have a friend in the business maybe they would be interested in owning part of the existing company.

All of these possible money suppliers will have different requirements for paying the money back. Make sure you can see your way clearly on how you will accomplish the repayment. This business can be adversely affected by interest rates so you would need a second way to make the payments.

A person thinking about ownership in this field must remember that it can be feast or famine as far as sales and commissions go. This is not like being in the restaurant business or owning a printing company. Successful brokers can make considerable money in a good market. They can also have periods that are very tight as to sales. So, having a high risk-tolerance and the ability to flow with the changes is essential. If you are rigid or have an easy panic button, this direction of career is NOT for you.

The brokers which tend to succeed have a policy of putting away some of their earnings during good times to cover the less profitable times. Doing this just shows the broker has a realistic view of the business and a long term plan. Either you are planning to succeed or you are planning to fail. Thinking that the sun will continue to shine on your business is a naïve view which will come back to haunt you.

Conclusions

The real estate business can be extremely profitable during low interest rate economies. The legal and state requirements make the ownership of a brokerage firm more difficult to own than with other businesses. Buying and selling a real estate business is somewhat more difficult due to the restrictions that are placed on the owner of a real estate firm because a broker of record is necessary.

You must have the appropriate licenses in place before you can begin operation. This is true whether you buy a company or start one up from scratch. Finding a firm you can afford will take some time and research on your part. Hiring a professional business broker may speed up the search.

Deciding early on if you want to be a specialist will set other decisions in place. Niche areas that you are an expert in will help cut the competition somewhat.

A general real estate business will have the potential for more clients but will need and ongoing advertising campaign to gain listings and clients looking to buy. The start-up is cheaper to open, but will have little cash flow like an existing firm. Money flow is the one huge advantage buying an existing business for the new owner.

Paul D. Kings

CHAPTER 5 - TIPS FOR MAKING A GOOD REAL ESTATE BUSINESS PLAN

Why Invest in Real Estate?

Real estate offers alot of investment opportunities. A large amount of money may be needed to get into a real estate business. Building your cash savings and reserves is a must. You are unlikely to risk your entire life savings if you make an investment in this field. The return increases in time and do not diminish if you invest wisely. The return is generally proportional to the risk you are willing and able take.

Investing in real property is one of the most complicated business activities, but can be so rewarding in the long run. The fact is, this is a well known investment vehicle specifically designed for middle and upper class investors. Most who have tried doing investment in real-estate have found investing in property very rewarding, but even renovating a house (flipping) or managing a rental property can take alot of work.

Real estate investment is something that you should think about carefully. Do not just get yourself into it unless you know that you can effectively handle it. Investing in property, whether for selling or rental purposes, is something that you can learn either by becoming a broker, a partner or through the school-of-hard-knocks. However, learning how to make an investment is not a simple and easy procedure if you are just trying to 'wing it' by yourself.

You should be aware that if you are new, there are lot of surprises that come along with setting up a real estate business, especially when it comes to purchasing a property. Many complications and obstacles will come up, so you have to be patient, flexible, and able to strategize the process. Getting involved emotionally with a business transaction or a particular house is fatal to a real estate business.
Initially, you have to determine what kind of property investment you wish to make prior to even searching for a house.

Among the most common investment property sources that you may consider include foreclosure sales (usually found through the court system), tax deeds, real estate agents, private sales and multiple listing services.

Once you have found a possible investment property, you should assess and verify its condition as a whole, because they are required to disclose any defect in the property that is not readily apparent. Then you can get an inspection, either a short inspection (with limited scope) or a full detailed inspection for high priced properties or if there is a concern raised with the seller. Speak with the property seller regarding the sale terms and possible price of the property.

Once an agreement has been reached between you and the seller, you can then ask for a sale contract. Bear in mind to never close a deal until both you and the buyer or renter are happy with the terms so that problems don't come up later on. Leaving a little room for negotiation later will relieve your mind if a cost crops up that you didn't expect, such as a lien or a permit issue.

There are different ways to earn money from the property you invest in. You may rent it out or live in it and let it appreciate in value by building equity over time. Rental properties are investments that can appreciate in value and the property can give you a great increase in earnings after few years if done wisely. Basically, you get a renter to pay your mortgage over time and you get the tax benefits until you sell it at the higher appreciated value later on. It is a win-win!

While real-estate can create long term income, as an investor, you should seek advice from an experienced partner who is capable of developing and delivering a successful strategy from experience. It takes a lot of conscientious work, strategy, and experience to make a full time investing career work for you.

Writing An Effective Business Plan

An effective business plan, for most business, can help you think about the business and get to know it fully. It also helps you to strategically plan for the different aspects of the business such as scalable growth and long-term equipment expenses. Such plans let the investor know what will be pursued as well as provide a clear road map for the management to follow.

Savvy investors always put together a business plan for each property investment. It is important therefore, that you take your time to plan each real estate investment you make.

In writing your plan, you have to identify the areas for improvement and the strategies for increasing the value of the property.

For first-time investors, it is important that you ask the following questions before writing your plan:

- Why am I going into real estate business?
- What challenges are involved in real estate?
- Can I handle these challenges with patience, flexibility, and risk tolerance?

If you are smart enough to do real estate, but you give yourself ulcers and insomnia about the risk, then it is not for you. I always gauge how I sleep as a perfect indication of how I am coping with a certain decision or path. Taking time to answer these questions may prevent you from making costly mistakes about your temperament, which make this type of investment a disaster for many people.

Real estate investment comes with its own challenges and it is important that you know them and have a plan for resolving each of them in a way that you can still rest at night. When you are planning on bringing in investors, they will ask to look at your business plan. The investors will want to see that you have experience in acquiring and managing real estate and have enough fortitude to face the challenges and changes ahead.

They want to know if you are emotionally and financially capable of handling tenants who do not pay and refuse to leave. Can you on the fifth day of the month turn every account which is not paid over to eviction attorneys, without a backward glance? Or, when someone calls you and says they are going to be five days late with their rent, do you skip them on the eviction list? If you do, then most of the time you will be left with an eviction later that will be more costly in rent lost and damages. Once the tenant eats through their security deposit, then they can do whatever they want without you having much power over them.

Your investors will want to know if you are capable of handling the strategic maintenance of the property and the contractors or vendors involved. Do you fall in love with a property and put in the kitchen that is YOUR dream kitchen? Or do you put in a kitchen that is serviceable and functional and clean, without any special bells and whistles? I can't even count how many tenants have destroyed high-end appliances which should not have been put in a rental.

Your business plan will include a business SWOT Analysis:
- **Strengths**: what you have going for your business...
- **Weaknesses**: what your business is lacking...
- **Opportunites**: where you can improve without lots of capital outlay....

- **Threats**: your weaknesses which would be too expensive to overcome, but your competition has already accomplished.

You many want to talk to local brokers who know the market and can give sincere and honest advice about these aspects of your business.

What about insurance and tax reporting? You must be able to source for the right insurance coverage on your property. You must make sure all dues are paid in taxes and your accounts balanced. If you are not very good at this, you may consider getting it done through consulting or a professional property manager.

Partnership is also an important issue in real estate investments. If you consider bringing in partners or investors, you have to look at securities law issues and investor communications. You must be ready to provide the reports and financials at intervals determined by the investors or according to your state's laws. Most investors like to see quarterly financial reports.

Writing an effective real estate business plan, even when you know about the business, helps you to know it better and put planning in place. Put yourself in the investors' shoes when writing your plan. Think about what they want to see and hear and address those issues in advance, so you look prepared for anything.

Above all, writing an effective real estate plan requires getting all the available information you need in putting the business together. Just that one act, if done with dedication, can be of benefit to your business because it will remind you to do things you may be neglecting.

More information about your business and its competition is always a good thing. Most business owners take the ostrich approach put their heads in the sand with any skill or issue they do not know how to deal with. In the age of YouTube and Google, you should be able to learn anything you want to for free, so don't be afraid of it or let it get worse before you solve the problem.

CHAPTER 6 - INVESTING IN COMMERCIAL PROPERTIES

Investing in Commercial Property

Investing in commercial property is a great way to invest your money. There are many alternatives to investing in commercial property which makes it good for every type of investor to get involved. So what are the options available for those interested in commercial property?

Some of the options you may already know exist, lets look at some:

Listed property trust is the simplest way to invest in commercial property. All you have to do is open an account with a stockbroker, deposit some money, and then place an order. Listed property trust can be found on the stock market. They invest in a wide range of commercial property i.e main office buildings, shopping centres, as well as industrial and leisure properties.

The trust manager chooses properties and is responsible for the maintenance, renovation, and for collecting rentals. Property securities are managed funds which invest in a list of property trusts.

This option is very good for somebody who is unsure which trust is appropriate. Purchase is through a prospectus, which is information about the investment which can guide you to know more about the investment's management, history, and potential income.

Another simple way to invest is public property syndicates, with application via a prospectus. The downfall is they require a large minimum outlay and you are locked into the investment for the duration of syndicate unless you can find someone to buy the investment from you.

If you have researched the market and have some acquired knowledge, then **direct property investment could be for you.** You can also buy direct property through a private property syndicate.

Mortgage funds are managed funds that lend money for investment property. The investor will be offered security and returns that are a little higher than a bank term deposit, but there are no capital gains. Commercial property is thought of as office, retail, and industrial location, but as an investor you need to be aware of the many options available to you.

Health care, child care, and retirement properties are great examples, also parking lots, storage facilities. An article read "Americans regard self storage as an absolute blue chip investment and is considered the safest real estate based investment in the United States."

So when is the right time to invest in commercial property? If you are a participant in the commercial share market you would be aware of the "investment clock." It's purpose is to show how the economic cycle works. A overheating economy is followed by higher interest rates and falling share prices, when the economy declines so does interest rates and shares begin to rise again.

Here is a guide to the way commercial property could fit with the economy:

The economy starts to slow. Direct properties stop rising and may even decline. The authorities inject liquidity (ready cash) into the economy. The stock market and listed property trusts rise. The economy begins to rise. Direct property begins to rise. Inflation may also rise and interest rates rise. Then stock market and listed property trusts fall.

American research has identified four phases based on economic and supply and demand:

- **Phase one** is when the market is generally in a condition of oversupply, due to a weak economy and too much construction from when the economy was strong. This is the bottom of the cycle. Vacancy rates will be high and rents would be falling. During this period new construction will cease, while demand slowly starts to grow again.

- **Phase two**, new spaces will continue to grow. There will be very little construction and rents rise sometimes sharply. This will cause developers once again initiating the construction of new buildings until there is an equilibrium between supply and demand.

- **Phase three**, demand continues to grow and supply grows faster. Rental growth could slow down.

- **The final phase** brings the market to a point of oversupply, due to over-building, with the condition aggravated by the economy weakening. Rents go down because of all of the vacancies; the building goes down because rents become cheaper than buying.

Tips for Buying Commercial Property

People who have had years of experience investing in commercial properties clearly suggest that it takes a willingness to spend a great amount of time and effort upfront in terms of researching, recognizing the best investments, and developing the right kinds of relationships. You can very easily think you are buying a great deal and get a real money pit. The more you know in this business, the safer your money will be.

Whether you are hoping to go straight into commercial property investments or you have experience investing in residential properties, you will want to familiarize yourself with these guidelines for success.

The first tip is to think big. It is not any more difficult to manage 50 apartment units than it is to manage 10 units. Plus, the more you buy, the less you will pay per unit. If the purchase of a 5-unit apartment complex requires you to get commercial financing, why would you even bother? Go big or go home.

Also, do not automatically choose apartments. While there is nothing wrong with investing in this kind of property, there are many other kinds of buildings to explore, such as office buildings, mobile homes, industrial buildings, and even land. Consider all the possibilities despite your comfort zone.

Having said that, you must be willing to take your time. This is where the patience factor comes into play with investing in these types of properties because commercial deals generally take longer to buy, have renovated, and sell than single-family homes. This is not intrinsically a bad thing, but you must be aware that rushing it could ruin a potentially great opportunity.

Because investing in this kind of properties costs more money than single-family homes, you may have no choice but to work with collaborators because you are not likely to qualify on your own. This is not a bad thing, since many of these properties are sold even though they were never formally listed. This means the more people you have in your network, the more deals you will be capable of finding. Plus, you will have a source to turn to for answers to any questions that might you have.

Finally, you will need to secure good financing ahead of time. Keep in mind that you will get a loan that is much larger when you are investing in commercial properties, which means you will have to put more money down or get your partner to do so. The main difference is that there is often no personal liability if the deal does not work out, giving you an added incentive to invest in commercial properties.

Why Invest in Commercial Properties?

There's no doubt that the residential real estate market is a profitable place to invest in, but with the current economic situation, it has been in a slump for quite some time now, but the commercial real estate market continues to thrive for a number of good reasons. In this chapter I will be sharing the top 5 reasons why investing in commercial properties is a great choice to build both your career and wealth.

1. Residential real estate properties are more common. Most of the home buyers and sellers have overlooked the many potential commercial deals. So if you enter the commercial real estate business, you will have less competition with more opportunities for you.

2. Commercial properties are not common and possess different features that can attract more buyers if only you know how to market them. If you don't, there are ways that you can learn them. Also, when placing a value to your commercial properties, you can do it differently from the way residential properties are valued. In commercial properties, the value is not fixed so you can always put an additional value to your property based on its highest and best use.

3. More people are curious about commercial properties. As I said earlier, residential properties are common which makes commercial ones appear different and are appreciated differently. Plus, if you have them in a developing country this could give you lots of opportunities. A developing country will be needing more commercial properties to house their growing businesses.

4. The potential of getting higher income and quicker returns is big. Compare to residential, the properties in commercial real estate earn more and earn fast. They generally provide significant financial benefits for the long-term.

5. You have more options in financing. There are many financing options where you can choose from which could make the task of starting the investment venture easy and less time-consuming. This is because there are now available programs made to help investors finance commercial investment. Between commercial mortgage bankers, hard money lenders, soft money lenders, and loans from other entities such as non-profits for revitalization, you should have many options for financing your commercial property.

It is a risky business venture because it involves more capital money. The properties involved are usually bigger than residential properties. It's generally worth the risks, especially since it gives a greater chance of attaining financial success. Not only can you create unlimited income potential with a great business plan, but you can also create long-term security of high returns on leases which range from 3 to 99 years in length.

Tips on How to Sell Commercial Properties

Selling a product is all about making a convincing case about its merits to potential buyers and creating marketing channels to bring buyers and sellers together. Commercial real estate sale requires systematic efforts on the part of the seller to reach a wider set of potential buyers. Marketing is the key aspect that needs to be focused upon.

How to Sell

Selling anything is about matching supply with demand. You need to identify people and businesses that would be interested in buying a particular piece of commercial property, which you are selling. Here are some marketing ideas for you, which will definitely help you cinch a deal.

Do Your Homework

Making a sale is all about tapping the right sales channels and reaching your target group of buyers. Before you can sell, you need to do your share of homework and research. First, study the property which you plan to sell. It may be a shop, office space, or a piece of land, which is ideally suited for a commercial complex.

Make a list of pros for a buyer, who would buy it and also list out the cons. Consider the location and identify the niche businesses that could take advantage of such a commercial space. The highest and best use would be determined for the property through an appraiser, so it may be a good time to get an expert's opinion.

If it's a shop in a business district, would a fast food chain be interested in buying it or would a clothing brand prosper there? Thinking on these lines will help you decide your marketing strategy to reach niche buyers who would be interested in it. Make an information brochure with all the details about the property, including square footage, amenities, and the nearest landmarks to its location. Last, you need to research the market prices in the area, which will help you determine what would be a reasonable price for the property.

Advertise in Newspaper Classifieds

One of the best ways to get the word across, about your commercial property is to advertise in a newspaper or online outlet. Provide all the vital details, along with the location details.

Let the advertisement be well designed and have a catchy line like 'Ideal Space For a Boutique' or 'Prime Location For a Fast Food Restaurant.' This advertisement will definitely get you some serious inquiries. Expect lot of calls and arrange for somebody to take them on a tour of the property for you.

Post Ads on Real Estate Portals

Another way of advertising your commercial property for sale is to post information about it on real estate portals that have a national and international exposure. Provide detailed information about the property site, along with photos, with contact details. This is bound to generate a lot of inquiries.

Publicize Through a Sales Billboard

One of the most conventional ways of advertising your property is to put a 'For Sale' billboard near it, which can catch the eyes of people visiting the area. You will be surprised to know how many properties have been sold through inquiries generated through simple billboards.

Create a Brochure and Pamphlets

If you want, you can even create brochures and pamphlets which can be mailed to prospective businesses who might be interested in them. This can net in a lot of potential buyers from niche businesses.

Find a Real Estate Agent

You always have the option of leaving the whole job of advertising and finding buyers to a real estate agent, who will do it for a sales commission. In case you don't have the time or energy to go through the entire property advertising and follow-up campaign, agents can handle it all for you. They can also interface with the title company which will handle all the paperwork involved in closing a deal.

Research the track record of an agent before handing over your property to him for sale. You don't want your time to be wasted.

It is good to have a clear idea about the price which you, as a seller have in mind, before you start negotiating with a potential buyer. Decide on what your first selling price is going to be and how much are you willing to reduce your price if the buyer plays hardball. That is, be clear about the bargain price which you are willing to settle for.

Bring your negotiating skills to the fore, be reasonable and close the deal on your terms. Most importantly, don't let ego or 'winning' interfere with the numbers. Even if you won the negotiation, but you lost on the deal, it is not a win.

Real estate negotiation is a very complicated skill. It takes years to understand how to get to a 'yes' without being so difficult to work with that no one wants to do business with you. You have to be part psychologist, conflict manager, negotiator, and part best friend.

If you can balance all of those skills, the other side will want to close the deal with you. And maybe do business with you in the future. If you have a short minded view, you may get this deal done today at such a cost to the relationship that you spoil any future business opportunities.

So, the answer is to take the long view. If you are a professional, respectful, consider the needs of others, deal honestly with them; if they feel kindly toward you, then you will excel in this business. You will get multiple referrals of deals before they hit the market and people will rush to do business with you.

I would suggest that you try selling the property on your own first and if you don't find any suitable buyers after persistent effort, then go to an agent. If you manage to sell it all by yourself, you can save on the commission fees that are normally paid to agents. The key to selling is persistence and using as many sales channels as you can to reach the target pool of buyers.

Paul D. Kings

CHAPTER 7 - REAL ESTATE AGENTS

Who Are Real Estate Agents?

Real estate agents are professionals instrumental in connecting the buyer with the seller. Additionally, many real estate agents manage rentals wherein they introduce tenants to landlords and oversee the maintenance of the property on behalf of the landlords. In most areas real estate agents are required to be highly educated, licensed and are regulated by a governing body. Some real estate agents are also Realtors.

To use the title Realtor, a real estate agent must be a member of the National Association of Realtors which in addition to a number of other requirements, requires Realtors to adhere to a strict code of ethics and offers Realtors additional educational and designation opportunities. Though not required by rule or law, it might be a wise decision to seek the services of a bonafide Realtor. Usually, someone who is a Realtor is likely to stay in the business and learn their trade and is less likely to be doing real estate as a hobby. There's no worse feeling than putting hundreds of thousands of dollars in the hands of someone who is going to manage your transaction two hours per night and on weekends.

What Do Real Estate Agents They Do?

Real estate agents bring together two or more interested parties, perform those steps necessary to successfully conclude a transaction and charge a commission for their services.

For sales transactions, they charge commission to the seller while for rentals, commission is typically charged the landlord. Real estate agents generally calculate their fee as a percentage of the selling price (in the case of a sale) and as part of the rent for rental units.

How Do Real Estate Agents Do Their Job?

People who want to sell or rent their property leave details of their property with the real estate agent. Along with all property details the real estate agent will typically have keys to the house to facilitate showings or put a lock box on the door to allow other realtors to access it for showings. The other interested party (i.e. the buyer/tenant), gets access to this information and to the property by contacting the real estate agent.

That's how the real estate agent becomes a hub of information. Contrary to some common misconceptions, real estate agents typically represent the seller or the buyer, but rarely both because it is against most state laws.

Why Should I Use A Real Estate Agent?

First and foremost, to protect yourself. Real estate transactions are highly regulated, highly paper (document) intensive transactions. The real estate agent possesses an in-depth knowledge of the laws, rules, regulations, disclosures and documentation necessary to successfully complete the transaction to the satisfaction of the buyer, the seller and the law.

Because real estate agents are most familiar with local real estate market conditions, it is wise and makes sense to seek the advice of an agent to get an idea of the current trends and pricing for properties within that market. A professional, full-time real estate agent will know the prices (or price range) of various properties of different types and at various locations within the region.

Because of the real estate agent's knowledge and expertise, property sellers often get a few thousand dollars more for their property.

Many home seekers, including seasoned real estate investors use the services of real estate agents to locate the best real estate bargains in the easiest and quickest manner. Agents often know deals which are coming up on the market before they get there, which can save you money and time.

Furthermore, the best agents analyze the wants and needs of a home buyer/tenant and provide valuable input as to the kinds of properties available to them within their budget. Therefore, a good real estate agent will not just present a list of available properties to the buyer/tenant but will actually discuss their needs and make suggestions. They have resources to check background, credit, and criminal factors which would be cost prohibitive for you to do.

The good real estate agent, working in this manner benefits in at least two ways. First and most obviously, when the real estate agent is able to successfully complete the transaction the commission is earned and the real estate agent is paid. Secondly, if they make the customer/client happy they earn a good reputation and often receive referrals (hence more business).

It is worth noting that there is a myth floating around that real estate agents only work on behalf of the seller, buyer beware.

This is not written in stone nor is it always the case. Real estate agents are, in most regions, highly regulated.

With few exceptions, real estate agents work either for the seller (as is the case with many listing agents) or for the buyer (as is the case for a buyer's agent). Their responsibility is to act as the 'agent' for whom they are representing. Which means that they act in your best interests and do not do or say anything that is not in your best interest.

Additionally, some areas allow for dual agency where an agent can work for both the seller and the buyer or as a transaction broker where the agent represents the transaction itself and neither the seller nor buyer individually. However, in the case of dual agency/transaction brokerage, note that rule, regulation (law) and ethics do not permit the agent to act in favor of either party while in detriment to the other. If you are unsure of the relationship between you and your real estate agent, do not hesitate to ask.

There's always the choice of having your agent act as a single agent, which means they act as if they are your agent to get the deal done. They are not allowed or obligated to 'play fair' with the other agent. They have to be honest, but they do not disclose anything to the other agent without your WRITTEN approval.

It is a much closer relationship than any other. They are an extension of you. They can't act in their best interests. They can't do anything without your expressed wishes, so they perform at the highest fidelity to what you ask of them.

What Buyers and Sellers Should Know

Buyers specifically should follow the **Ten Rules of Buying a Home**:

- Don't make changes to your job. Don't quit, get fired, change jobs, or become self-employed.
- Don't buy a car, truck or van, unless you plan on living in it.
- Don't significantly change the balances on your credit lines or let any of them lapse.
- Don't spend the money that you have set aside for closing on a vacation, then try to bargain that the real estate agents decrease their commission to make the deal happen.
- Don't lie on your loan application or forge documents. It will be discovered.
- Don't buy furniture, lawn equipment, or anything that you have to store for months as the closing gets delayed due to rules 1-5.

- Don't have every store that offers you 20% off your purchases that day check your credit, making a string of suspicious credit inquiries before closing.
- Don't make large deposits or withdrawals from your accounts without clearing them through the loan officer.
- Don't change banks that you do business with or bank accounts in the middle of a transaction.
- And please, do not put your name and your credit at risk for your kid, grandkid, sister, mother, father, grandfather, or whoever.

If you break any one or more of these rules, you are not going to get to closing. Almost 10% of transactions fail for one of these ten reasons. Just don't do it. If in doubt, ask your Realtor or mortgage broker.

Basically, during the transaction until after it has closed, do NOT change anything about your life. A bonus rule: do not get a divorce during the time you are waiting for the transaction to close. I can't explain how much havoc it will cause.

For most buyers and sellers, the prospect of dealing with a real estate agent brings forth unknown fears. While some agents are genuine and reputable and consider their clients best interest as their top priority, there are unscrupulous or irresponsible individuals who are just trying to make a quick buck at someone else's expense.

As a buyer or sellers of a property, it is your responsibility to choose a estate agent prudently. So, here is a look at what you should know about real estate agents before you approach one.

Depending on which side they are working for (the buyers or the sellers), the realtor acts as an intermediary between the buyer and the seller and helps to complete the sale of a property. For their services, they are offered a commission from the transaction. If you trace the money, it is from the buyer that the agent is paid, because the buyer has to buy the property at a high enough amount to cover the seller's needs plus the commission or the deal will not be made. **So, even though the physical payer of the commission is the seller at the closing table, the money was generated from the buyer.**

When working on behalf of the seller, the agent is responsible for putting the details of a property in the Multiple Listing Service (MLS) for the area and undertaking other efforts such as home staging to market the property. They may suggest certain repairs or decluttering be done before you list the property. Just because you are in love with the home, this doesn't mean you can leave out these important details.

In case of a residential property, a real estate agent may start off by putting up the details of the property on their personal or company website depending on whether they are a part of a realtor firm or work on their own. Then there are over 200 websites that most realtors feed or syndicate their rental listings to.

Some of them are automatic with MLS and some are extra services the Realtor will have connected themselves to. If you find an agent which is not syndicating their listings, then you should move on to someone who does. Most buyers and renters start their search online.

Besides marketing the property, the agent who lists your home is also responsible for following up with other agents who might have clients that may have expressed interest in the property. An agent is also supposed to help you negotiate the best deal possible. He/She is with you every step of the way until the home is sold; advising you on all matters including procuring the services of a lawyer or a closing agent.

The agent does not charge the client/home seller for his marketing efforts; however, you will have to incur any legal cost involved in the selling process, such as recording, document preparation, and closing fees. He coordinates with the real estate agent handling the property on behalf of the seller and arranges to show the premises to his clients.

A real estate agent from the buyer's side also helps to negotiate the best deal for his client and is with the buyer through out the purchasing process. When working from the buyers's side, a realtor is responsible for rummaging through the property listings of an area that his client is interested in.

A real estate agent is also responsible for approaching a professional to get a property evaluation done. Some real estate agents may also offer other services such as advice and help for procuring home loans.

Real estate agents not only earn commission from the sale and purchase of homes but also when a property is leased. Usually the commission is paid to the real estate agent at the final settlement of the deal.

Who Should You Choose to be Your Real Estate Agent?

A real estate agent can be an intermediary on behalf of the seller or the buyer. When buying a house, it would be best to hire the services of an agent who can work on your side, the same holds true when selling a home as well; you would be better of approaching a real estate agent who works for sellers.

Although real estate agents who work from the sellers or the buyer's side do not have different credentials, some agents choose to play on a single turf while double agents may work for both the seller and the buyer simultaneously earning commissions from both.

The Sellers Real Estate Agent

An agent working on behalf of the seller will have his loyalty toward his client and he/she will try his best to convince the seller to give his client the best deal, which means the highest return on their investment, in the shortest time, with the lowest fees. So, as a buyer, if you were to ask the seller's agent if his client would accept a higher deal, he will be obligated to not divulge this information to you.

The Buyers Real Estate Agent

Similarly, agents who work on behalf of the seller owe their responsibility to their clients and will try to get their clients the best deal possible, which means the lowest price on the purchase, in the most reasonable time frame, long inspection times, and with the lowest buyer's side fees. So, if asked, the seller's agent will not be willing to offer information on how low their client will go in terms of the price. It takes a wily buyers agent to get that information out of them.

A Dual Agent

A dual agent is obligated to keep the honest picture in front of both parties; since he is entitled to a commission from both parties, he owes his loyalties to both the buyer and the seller.

Most real estate agents have a list of buyers as well as sellers so it is not unusual for an agent to work on behalf of both parties or at least get another agent from his real estate firm to negotiate on behalf of the seller or the buyer.

The Problem With Real Estate Agents

While real estate agents are in the business of marketing properties, it is not uncommon for them to play up their credentials. After all, it is a dog eat dog world and there is certainly no dearth of realtors in the market. While this is acceptable, some individuals resort to lying blatantly about their accomplishments and often their customers end up paying for their tall claims.

So, make sure that you check all the claims that are being made by a potential estate agent. Do not hesitate to ask for references or check their online reviews. If he has not mentioned his experience in the brochure, make it a point to ask him about it.

Also, inquire about other properties that he may have sold which were similar to the one that you want to sell/buy; this would include properties in the same area, of the same size and price range and check their online profiles with realtor.com, Zillow.com and others. Many review websites are linked directly to the Realtor's MLS page so you can see what closings they have done and what pending sales they have.

Finding a good and reliable agent can save you a lot of trouble while hanging out with the wrong guy can quickly turn into a nightmare so take your time when picking an agent to buy/sell your home.

How to Look For a Good Real Estate Agent

You may be planning to sell your home or buy a new home. Either way, you're probably looking for a great real estate agent, because you are entrusting a very large financial transaction in their hands.

Realtor, Real Estate Agent - is there a difference?

There are Realtors and there are real estate agents. These are not synonymous terms. A real estate agent is licensed to "represent a buyer or a seller in a real estate transaction in exchange for commission." Real estate agents typically work for a real estate broker, who has taken additional training and exams to be able to run a real estate office.

A Realtor also is licensed and may sell real estate as either an agent or a broker. There are completely ethical real estate agents and Realtors. The primary difference is that a Realtor has made an additional commitment to honor the 17-article code and profession of the real estate business and paid a hefty fee for the privilege.

The Search and Some Questions

Looking for a great real estate agent means that you will be asking questions, so let's start building your list of questions:

Referrals

Ask your friends, colleagues, and relatives for referrals and then check those Realtors out online before you contact them. Most people who have had a positive experience working with a agent will gladly describe their experience and why they feel their agent was exceptional.

Referrals From Professionals

It is certainly appropriate to ask real estate agents for referrals. Financial institution representatives, especially mortgage brokers, are likely to be aware of exceptional agents.

Open Houses

Going to open houses is a great, non-threatening way to meet real estate agents. Pay attention to the agent's manners and appearance, his/her professionalism, and the quality of promotional material provided at the open house. Does the agent seem knowledgeable about the property and the local market? Is the agent ready to point out the home's features, or does he basically ignore visitors?

When you have a generally favorable impression of an agent, be sure to collect a business card and make notes of your observations.

References

Plan to interview several agents before making a decision and signing a buyer's agreement. During the interview, ask each candidate to provide referrals of recent clients and call those referrals. What are the asking and selling prices of their properties? How long the home was on the market?

Take time to look up the estate board of licensing services to confirm that the candidate is currently licensed and whether any complaints or disciplinary actions have been filed against the agent.

Experience

How long has the agent been in business? You should be looking for the agent who thoroughly knows the local market in which you are selling or planning to buy your home. It takes time to build expertise and market knowledge. One agent recommends that any viable candidate should have at least five years' experience.

Is the agent full or part-time?

You should expect, and ask for, a full time agent. Hobby agents are more likely to make friends than to complete sales.

Next steps

When evaluating the qualifications of real estate agents, look at their websites and current listings. Your future agent should be web and technology savvy, using all current media to help you find your perfect home or sell your current one. The agent should also be able to communicate reliably and regularly using the form(s) of contact you prefer - fax, phone, text, or e-mail.

Ideally, your prospective agent is busy but not too busy to effectively represent you. Most full-time agents can handle twenty transactions simultaneously. When they have that many transactions, they usually begin to build a team. If you feel that the candidate is not committed to giving your sale or purchase full and enthusiastic service, then move on.

Your agent should be realistic about pricing, marketing, and representing you as the seller or buyer. "If it sounds too good to be true..." can apply to real estate agents and services, too. Trust your powers of observation and intuition. When you combine them with the information you have gathered from your interviews, you will be ready to make a well-informed decision.

Benefits of Using a Real Estate Agent

Purchasing or selling a home is typically the largest investment most people will make in their lives. Whether you're buying a new home or selling your existing home, a real estate agent can help protect your interests and potentially save you a substantial amount of money. We have compiled a list of benefits for both the homebuyer and seller.

Reasons Why You Should Use a Real Estate Agent When Buying a Residential or Commercial property

1. It is a misnomer that a home buyer is not required to pay the real estate agent. When a real estate agent represents a home buyer on a purchase of a home, the commission earned by that agent is paid for out of the proceeds of the closing. The commission is taken out of the sales price, which is paid by THE BUYER of the home. So, the buyer pays the home's value plus commission and fees and the seller turns around and pays it to the real estate agent. It is inaccurate to think that the buyer does not pay the commission. If the buyer did not pay more than the home was worth, i.e. the commission, then the seller would not sell the home.

2. Real estate agents can choose to have access to the Multiple Listing Service (MLS). The MLS is a service that the real estate agent pays for which provides them the most up to date information on homes that are for sale in your area.

This service is not available to the general public, but the agent can do many things to keep you up to date, such as providing you with a MLS searchable app or a link to their website which may have a widget that links to their MLS.

With the MLS an agent can find out information about the home like taxes, how long it has been listed, price changes, special features on the home as well as home sales trends etc.

3. Real Estate Agents have knowledge about the area and the factors which affect home prices and desirability, such as roads which may be getting upgrades or businesses which are going to start. A real estate agent should also be able to tell you about the neighborhood, schools, activities, recreational areas, etc. that are available in the areas that you are looking to purchase.

4. Real Estate Agents know how to negotiate with the seller on your behalf. Negotiating the price of a home can often get very difficult. In a seller's market, it is uncommon to ask for closing costs to be paid, repairs to be completed, home warranties, or inspections because there are dozens of buyers for each home on the market. In a buyer's market, the seller will likely use closing costs, repair credits, home warranties, or prepaid inspections as lures to get a specific buyer to buy their home.

Your real estate agent will know how much inventory is on the market at any one time, so they will be able to guide you if it is a seller's versus buyer's market.

Often real estate agents are able to negotiate items in the home like washers/dryers, refrigerators, or furniture into the sale of the property. Your real estate agent's job is to make sure you get the best deal.

5. Agents keep the deal going. Once your offer has been accepted you will have lot of tasks that need to be completed in a short amount of time. Right on your purchase contract, you will see all the deadlines in writing, such as an inspection within two weeks of the acceptance of the purchase offer. Your agent can help you keep track and orchestrate all the tasks required in the buying process.

Reasons To Use a Real Estate Agent When Selling Your Home or Commercial property

1. A real estate agent is worth the commission. Once you actually consider all the things your agent will do for you from the time they list the home to the time it sells, the commission paid to that agent is usually money well spent. Often times an agent will be able to help you get your home sold much faster and for more money than you could have on your own.

2. Agents understand the current housing market. Choose an agent that lives in your area. This agent will understand the neighborhood, home values, benefits of the area, and the local competition.

3. Agents know how to sell your home. This is their job, and just like any other job, if they don't do a good job they get fired. A real estate agent is a professional and should know what they are doing. It is often a good idea to get an agents track record prior to letting them sell your home. Selling any home takes experience, dedication and knowledge in this market. Their job is to attract buyers and sell the home.

4. Agents know what will make houses sell. Your agent will be able to give you advice on what could be done to the home to get it sold more quickly. Anything from staging the home to making minor repairs or upgrades.

5. Agents will put your home on the MLS. A real estate agent has access to the Multiple Listing Service (MLS). This tool is only available to real estate agents and allows them to get your home in front of thousands of other agents and buyers.

6. Agents know how to market your home. Your agent will know what to do to market your home for sale, whether that is an open house, internet exposure, flyers, caravans, etc.

7. Agents represents you to the end. Your agent will represent you from the time the home is listed to the time it closes escrow. An agent's job is to make sure your interests are protected in the sale of the home and everything negotiated in the contract is fulfilled. If a problem arises at or after closing, your agent is there to help resolve any issues.

8. Agents will keep the sales process on track so that any deadlines in the Sales Contract are met on time and you don't lose the sale. Many For-Sale by Owners neglect timelines and the sale is canceled by the buyer, which returns the earnest money deposit.

9. Agents will be able to negotiate the best terms for your home, including perks to the sale, timelines which are more favorable to you, strict buyer obligations, that the buyer shares any inspections or appraisals with you, and many other items which add up to your benefit.

Paul D. Kings

WANT TO LEARN MORE?

Get my book called:

"Investing for Beginners -
Learn About Personal Finance, Real Estate Investing, Money Making Opportunities, and Business Investing Success"

You will learn about:

- **Personal finance** understanding your cash flow and by creating opportunities to make more money than you spend.
- **Real estate investing** by knowing when and how to decide to hire a real estate agent and how to do real estate investing on your own.
- **Online money making machine** by knowing the most efficient way to make money online.
- **Business investing** so that you have a successful business, which brings you maximum income with the least amount of effort.

ABOUT THE AUTHOR

Paul D. Kings is a Software Engineer, Father, husband, and self-published author. He likes to write about selling and making money online. Paul has been selling on eBay and Amazon since 2007.

Do you want to read my new books for free?

Become a member of my ARC (Advanced Reader Copy) Team, and get my books for free before they are published on Amazon. Find out more at:

http://bit.ly/pauldkings

ONE LAST THING...

If you enjoyed this book or found it useful, I'd be very grateful if you'd post a short review on Amazon. Your support really does make a difference, and I read all the reviews personally so I can get your feedback and make this book even better.

Thanks again for your support!

www.ingramcontent.com/pod-product-compliance
Lightning Source LLC
Chambersburg PA
CBHW020922180526
45163CB00007B/2845